THE
ULTIMATE
GUIDE TO
TIKTOK

ISBN 978-1-338-73241-2

10 9 8 7 6 5 4 3 2 1   20 21 22 23 24

Printed in the U.S.A.   40
First edition 2020

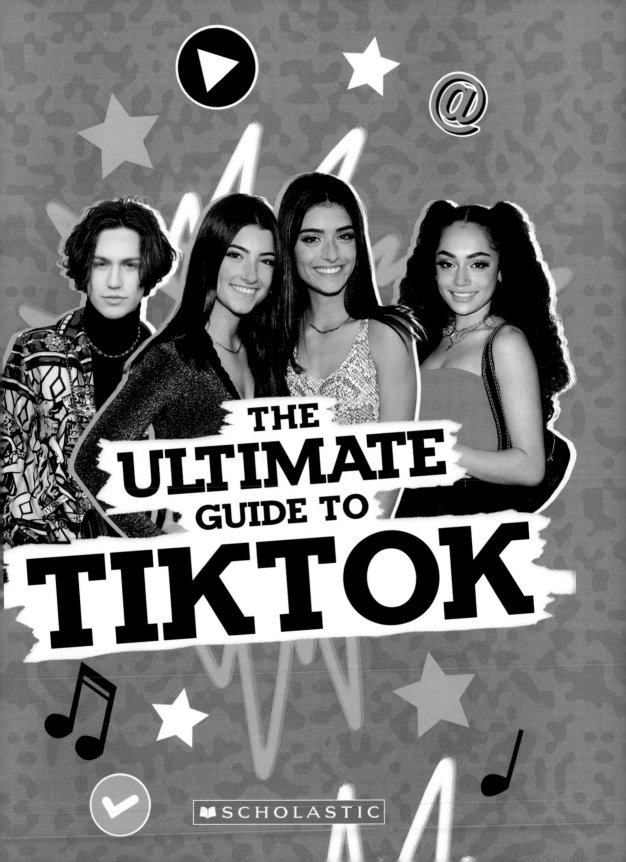

THE ULTIMATE GUIDE TO TIKTOK

SCHOLASTIC

CONTENTS

WELCOME!

This is your one-stop guide to the wonderful world of TikTok. Inside you'll hang out with creators like Charli D'Amelio, Jacob Sartorius, and Holly H. From info on how the app's biggest stars made their mark to the coolest collaborations, this book has it all.

THERE'S SO MUCH TO DISCOVER IN THIS AWESOME TIKTOK GUIDEBOOK!

Fan Favorites

Check out the profile pages for fun facts about your favorite stars!

Hot Tips

Learn how to create the perfect TikTok video so you'll be camera-ready in no time!

Sneak Peek

Get the lowdown on what happens in Hype House — the most talked about house on TikTok!

Statement Style

Use your talents and super skills to create your very own TikTok style.

WHAT ARE YOU WAITING FOR?

Turn the page to take the first step toward TikTok stardom!

IT'S **TIKTOK** TIME!

Are you a TikTok newbie?
Here's all you need to know about
one of the most exciting apps around.

The Basics

TikTok is an app and social channel for sharing amateur videos. Users create, edit, and share 15-second videos with their followers. The best clips are usually set to music! People follow a mix of their own friends and family, plus celebs.

History of TikTok

The video-sharing app started in China. TikTok very quickly gained hundreds of millions of followers. Originally called Musical.ly, it was released in 2014 and evolved to become TikTok in 2017. By 2019, TikTok had been downloaded over a billion times.

Who Uses the App?

Mostly Gen Z — TikTok has more young users compared to other social media sites like Facebook and Instagram. You must be age 18 or over to use the app! If you're under age 18, be sure to get your parent's permission before using TikTok.

NOT 18? If you are under the age of 18, never fear — this book will give you all you need to know to perfect your TikTok skills so that when that big birthday comes around, you will be ready to go!

Good Vibes Only

Lots of social media platforms are criticized for being negative, but on TikTok, comments are often positive and encourage empowerment.

Challenges and Hashtags

TikTok is all about the challenges and hashtags. They're a great way to find inspiration for the videos you want to make. Plus, it's always cool to see how a challenge evolves as different people show their own unique personalities in their videos.

LEARN THE LINGO

To understand TikTok, you need to know the slang. Here are a few basic terms that will come up again and again.

DUET — If you follow someone and they follow you back, you can make a TikTok together, no matter how far apart you are. Simply click the "Share" button, select "Duet," and record a killer video.

CRINGE — Cringe videos typically refer to someone acting awkwardly or in an embarrassing fashion while attempting to perform. Now, however, people have embraced the fun of making cringe-inducing content and duets. Users even record reaction videos to whatever they're doing.

CHALLENGES — TikTok thrives on challenges, and they are an easy way for people on TikTok to feel like they're part of the community. TikTok users will all make videos attempting to do the same thing, like the stair step challenge, where people dance up a set of stairs in an elaborate way.

FUN FACT: Some of the most popular memes started out on TikTok!

STAY SAFE

TikTok is lots of fun, but it's important to stay savvy when using the internet and social media apps.

Check the Rules

Always be sure to read the Terms of Use and Privacy Policy of any social media platform you want to use, including TikTok's. You should check the age limit of any website that you're planning to use. TikTok's terms and conditions say that users must be at least 18 years old before creating an account or using the app in any way. TikTok will delete the accounts of any users under 18.

Permission First

Before going online, always ask a parent or guardian for their permission and then agree on basic ground rules. It's important that they are involved in your plans to help keep you safe.

Ready to Share

If you have an account and you're excited about making your first video, hold on! Show it to a trusted adult before you post it. Remember to make sure that your posts don't reveal personal information that could put you in danger. Never give away your full name, address, phone number, or school details to anyone online. Never share posts that may give away details of where you live or where you go to school, such as a video of you in your school uniform.

Public Posts

If you're planning on posting cringe-worthy clips, remember that once your TikTok post has been made public, you cannot control what others do with it or say about it. If you wouldn't be happy with your mom or your little brother viewing any video you create, don't make it public.

Speak Up

Always speak to a trusted adult if you see or hear any posts or comments that upset you or make you feel uncomfortable. If you read anything mean or threatening that has been written about you, close the app and tell a trusted adult what has happened.

Be Kind

TikTok is all about having fun and being creative. You might not always like a post, but it's important to be kind. TikTok users found to be posting mean or offensive comments will have their accounts deleted.

Coins

TikTok Coins are used to buy things within the app, such as Diamonds or emojis to show other users that you like their work! Remember that Coins cost real money, so always get permission from your parent or guardian before purchasing.

Family Safety Mode

TikTok's Family Safety Mode is a way that your parent(s) or guardian(s) can link their TikTok account to yours. This means that your trusted grown-up can make sure that your safety settings are all correct and that you only see posts that are suitable for you. Remember that it's important not to spend too much time on TikTok. Make time to be with family and friends face-to-face, too.

PRIVACY, PLEASE!

Set your TikTok account to private so only your friends can find you online. You can follow TikTok's biggest stars, but don't speak to other users unless you know them in real life.

To make your account private, go to your settings on your profile page and switch on the "Private Account" button. Setting your account to private gives you control over who can see your videos.

To hide your location while using TikTok, go to the settings page and switch on the "Hide Location" button. This will stop the app from publishing where you are when you post a video or comment.

MEET @CHARLIDAMELIO

Charli D'Amelio soared to fame after joining TikTok in 2019 because of her dance talent and endless creativity. In 2020, Charli became the first TikTok star to smash 50 million followers!

TIKTOK ACCOUNT: @charlidamelio
NAME: Charli D'Amelio
DATE OF BIRTH: May 1, 2004
NATIONALITY: American
STAR SIGN: Taurus
TALENT: dancing

VIRAL MOMENTS

When it comes to dance TikToks, Charli sets the bar high. Her Renegade dance is undoubtedly one of her most popular TikTok posts. After she shared her video, tons of users included the dance moves in their clips. But best of all, Charli met the creator of the Renegade dance trend, Jalaiah Harmon. Charli shared a video of them dancing together featuring the original choreography!

COLLABS

Some of Charli's biggest videos have been her collabs. In fact, her first viral post was her TikTok duet with Joy (@move_with_joy). After sharing the video, she gained tons of followers. And who saw the moment Charli danced with the legendary Jennifer Lopez? It was all part of a Super Bowl TikTok challenge. You've got to check it out!

SISTER, SISTER

Charli's big sis, Dixie, is also a famous TikTok star. The sisters look so similar that people often mistake them for being twins. Dixie mostly posts lip-syncing and dance videos, including cute collabs with Charli. But these two are not the only famous D'Amelios. Nope, everyone in the family is a social media influencers. What a creative family!

MEET @LILHUDDY

There are so many things to love about the fashion icon and lip-sync guru Lil Huddy!

TIKTOK ACCOUNT: @lilhuddy
NAME: Chase Hudson
DATE OF BIRTH: May 15, 2002
NATIONALITY: American
STAR SIGN: Taurus
TALENT: lip-syncing

SUCCESS STORY

His flawless lip-syncing skills are what first made Chase Hudson stand out on TikTok. Have you seen his Pitbull and Justin Bieber videos yet? If not, why not?! They're the ones that first earned him his millions of TikTok followers.

@ TALENT SCOUT

Lil Huddy is living the creator dream! He's part of the Hype House in a big way. In fact, he's a cofounder along with Thomas Petrou. There is no doubt that he knows how to spot the next big TikTok star, and he calls himself the Hype House talent scout!

The nickname "Lil Huddy" originated from his dad's nickname, Huddy. Too cute!

GOT THE EDGE

When it comes to fashion, Lil Huddy has a distinctive look. His signature style is chains, a baseball cap or beanie, and oversized clothing — inspired by Billie Eilish.

HYPE HOUSE

If you love TikTok, then you'll probably know about Hype House — the mansion that TikTok's biggest stars call home. So, what are you waiting for? Let's explore . . .

What Is the Hype House?

The house is in Los Angeles, California, and some of TikTok's most famous stars live there! The content creator collective was set up in 2019 to create even bigger viral moments. Sounds amazing, right? The Hype House has its own TikTok account with over 15 million followers and counting (@thehypehouse).

Who Will You Find There?

Behind the mansion's doors, you will find a big bunch of TikTok, YouTube, and Instagram influencers. Celeb residents have included the likes of Charli D'Amelio, who received the first hype — you go, girl!

Who Started It?

Chase Hudson and Thomas Petrou founded the Hype House. They wanted a house dedicated to making content — so, it's not all about having fun and partying. These guys are always on the lookout for new talent to join the Hype House.

Are There Any Rules?

Thomas Petrou is the oldest member of the group and the one who works out any house issues. All members of the Hype House are supposed to create at least three TikTok videos per day. That's a lot of content!

Is Hype House the Only TikTok Creator House?

While the Hype House may have started the trend, there are other TikTok houses out there. Other groups, such as the University of Diversity and the LGBTQ-focused group Cabin Six, have been holding auditions for their own content houses. Watch this space . . .

FAB FAVORITES

Ready for some fill-in fun? Grab a pen and share some info about your favorite TikTok stars!

My fave TikTok star is . . .

chra

The types of videos they create are . . . Choose from the list below, or write in your own.

○ comedy ○ lip-sync ⦿ dance

_____

Their best video so far is . . .

_____

_____

_____

18

Three of their other videos I like are . . .

1. _charli_

2. _____

3. _____

I love them because . . .

_____

I most want them to collaborate with . . .

_____

After reading this book, I will start
following . . .

_____

The TikTok star I want to know more
about is . . .

_____

THE BIG QUIZ

Find out whether you're already a TikTok superfan or if it's time to step up your game! Put your knowledge to the test with this epic quiz. Don't worry if you get stuck — the answers are all somewhere in this book!

1. What is the name of Charli D'Amelio's sister?

a) Trixie
b) Dixie
c) Dilly

2. What was TikTok originally called?

a) Musical.ly
b) Instagram
c) Myspace

3. What is the name of the collective started by Chase Hudson and Thomas Petrou?

a) Viral Venture
b) Hype House
c) Hype Squad

4. What is the first move of the Renegade dance?

a) Dab
b) Clap
c) Woah

5. Before finding TikTok fame, the Lopez Brothers were known for their . . .

a) Impressions
b) Dancing
c) Comedy

6. What is Lil Huddy's real name?

a) Chase Hudson
b) Jason Hudson
c) Lacy Hudson

7. Who received the first hype?

a) Dixie D'Amelio
b) Charli D'Amelio
c) Thomas Petrou

8. Which TikTok star is trained as a Level 9 gymnast?

a) Maverick Baker
b) Loren Gray
c) Avani Gregg

9. Which duo released a song called "The Way You Move" in 2018?

a) Cash and Maverick Baker
b) Sky and Tami Odin
c) The Stokes Twins

10. What is Loren Gray's dog named?

a) Smudge Pom
b) Frou Frou
c) Fudge Pom

MEET
@AVANI

Meet the gymnast and dancer responsible for #ClownCheck! There is **SO** much to love about Avani.

TIKTOK ACCOUNT: @avani
NAME: Avani Gregg
DATE OF BIRTH: November 23, 2002
NATIONALITY: American
STAR SIGN: Sagittarius
TALENTS: gymnastics, dancing,
          and comedy

KNOWN FOR . . .

If it's challenges, comedy, and dance videos you're after, then Avani is your go-to gal. Her iconic #ClownCheck videos are a combination of Avani's makeup mastery and grumpy clown comedy skits. It didn't take long for her content to grab tons of attention and millions of followers. It's no wonder that Avani received her verification crown and style guru badge!

STUNTS

Did you know that Avani competed as a Level 9 gymnast? Seriously cool! Check out her TikTok channel to see some of her skillful stunts.

THE BIG TIME

In 2019, Avani joined stars like Charli D'Amelio and became part of one of the coolest collectives on the planet. Yep, you guessed it: the Hype House. With videos that just keep getting better, Avani delights her ever-growing fan base with her unique talents.

ON SET

When it comes to making videos, it's a good idea to choose your location carefully and prepare the space before you begin. Here are some tips for getting the set of your video just right!

⭐ LIGHT AND BRIGHT

Find a spot where there is plenty of light. Nobody wants to perform the perfect routine only to realize that they can't be seen in the recording! Experiment with flashlights or lamps in your films.

Need inspiration? Try following some stars from this book to see where they set their videos. You may find some cool ideas for where to film yours.

⭐ TIME TO TIDY

Clean up your space and do a quick check of your set before you hit "Record." You don't want to share anything embarrassing with the world.

⭐ WOBBLE WORRIES

Find somewhere safe to set your device while you record your video. You don't want a cracked screen! If you are doing a dance, make sure you have a steady spot for your camera, or if you want to make your video even more professional, consider buying a tripod.

SPACE OUT

Make sure you record your videos somewhere with enough space to move around freely. You can put your all into it without the fear of breaking anything. Don't just stick to indoors — try exploring outdoor locations, too.

HAVE FUN

Experiment with filters and special effects to get the best out of your set. A fun filter can brighten things up, and you only need to share the stuff that you want, so don't worry if it doesn't go as planned the first time around.

Always talk to a parent or guardian before going outside to make a video.

COLORFUL CREATIONS

It's all about color coordination. If you're wearing the same color clothes as your backdrop, you may just become a floating head. Try to wear contrasting colors to make yourself pop!

YOU STAR!

Your TikTok is all about you, so make sure you're the main focus.

And remember, don't overthink it — some of the best videos happen when you're being spontaneous.

Want to create a longer video? No problem! You can tag videos together in "stories" to create 60-second-long footage.

MEET ✓ @MAVERICKBAKER

Maverick: the uber-talented
lip-syncing, dancing ball of energy!

TIKTOK ACCOUNT: @maverickbaker
NAME: Maverick Baker
DATE OF BIRTH: December 13, 2000
NATIONALITY: American
STAR SIGN: Sagittarius
TALENTS: comedy and lip-syncing

FINDING FAME

Instagram is where Maverick first gained a following. Today, he's most famous for his lip-sync videos — they're the reason he's gained millions of followers. If you haven't seen one before, then you're in for a treat. One of his most viewed videos involves him and his brother, Cash, lip-syncing to LoCash's song "I Love This Life."

FAMOUS FAMILY

Maverick isn't the only internet-famous Baker. Maverick creates a lot of cool content with Cash — check out the baby Baker's TikTok: @cash.baker. Maverick's big sister, Lani Lynn, is a blogger and model — you can find her on TikTok, too: @lani.baker.

SEEING DOUBLE

In 2018, Cash and Maverick released their first song together, called "The Way You Move." People often mix the boys up — they look so similar, it's easy to see why!

MEET ✓
@LORENGRAY

If you want inspo from the best, then look
no further than megastar Loren Gray.

Loren has a dog
named Smudge
Pom. Super cute!

TIKTOK ACCOUNT: @lorengray
NAME: Loren Gray Beech
DATE OF BIRTH: April 19, 2002
NATIONALITY: American
STAR SIGN: Aries
TALENTS: acting, singing, and dancing

HER JOURNEY

Loren first found fame through her Snapchat show, *Glow Up*, which was packed with beauty tutorials and positivity. After joining Musical.ly and gaining a large following, she began to get bullied at school. Loren moved to LA and started a new life, growing her other social media platforms. These days, she is living the LA dream as an influencer.

MAKING IT BIG

At 17, Loren was the most followed person on TikTok. The social media star and Gen Z icon has followings in the millions across YouTube and Instagram, and a loyal fanbase called the Angel Squad.

MUSIC CAREER

Loren has been producing music since 2017. She signed with Virgin Records in 2018 and released her debut single, "My Story," later that year. As well as making her own music, in 2020, Loren made a cameo in Taylor Swift's video for "The Man."

29

GET THE LOOK

Want to look on point in your videos?
Check out these tips to help you create a
signature style that you'll love.
Get ready to stand out!

Nail It

Give your nails the all-star treatment. After all, they play a
big part in TikTok videos, with all those hand gestures. You
could choose a signature color that you always stick to, or
you could mix it up each time you post.

- comedy — go for rainbow nails
- lip-sync — something subtle
- collabs — coordinate your look

Hair Hype

The best hairstyle depends on the effect that you want
to achieve. If you have long locks, you may want to put
your hair back so it doesn't distract you from your routine.
Or perhaps you want your hair to swish as you move
for some added drama. Wigs are also a great way to
experiment without changing your own hair.

Block or Prints

When it comes to outfits, go with the stuff you feel most confident in. Remember, it's all about being yourself. Block colors tend to look better on camera compared with busy patterns like stripes. You can always test it out before you post!

Makeup Marvels

When you're starting out on TikTok, it's cool to stick with your usual makeup routine — don't feel pressured to change your look! And if you normally don't wear any makeup, then don't feel like you have to. If you'd like to try a bolder look, how about adding a classic eyeliner flick or testing some shimmer to catch the light?

Threads

Whether it's dressing up or dressing down, wear whatever makes you feel confident and comfortable. Making a TikTok in your school uniform or logo shirt is a big no-no. Those can reveal the name and location of your school, which are personal details you shouldn't give out publicly online. Change into your fave clothes that don't share personal info, and then start creating!

MEET @RIYAZ.14

"LIVING THE DREAM!"

"SMILE FOR THE CAMERA!"

#TIKTOKINDIA

He's one of India's most famous fashion influencers. It's time to find out more about the unstoppable Riyaz!

TIKTOK ACCOUNT: @riyaz.14
NAME: Riyaz Afreen
DATE OF BIRTH: September 14, 2003
NATIONALITY: Indian
STAR SIGN: Virgo
TALENTS: acting, modeling,
and lip-syncing

POSITIVE MESSAGE

You may know this talented TikTok star by his nickname, Riyaz Aly. And there is a lot to love about India's hottest teen icon. He's all about connecting with fans and spreading positivity. In fact, he has a pretty awesome motto: "Create a life you are obsessed with." Could you love him more?

GET SNAPPY

Besides having an eye for fashion, Riyaz is also a model, and he seriously loves photo shoots. When you check out his social media feed, it's easy to see why Riyaz has such a massive following as a fashion blogger and influencer — the camera loves him!

#DUETWITHRIYAZ

Riyaz loves collaborating with stars and fans on his videos. He's even got his own hashtag for when he does this: #DuetWithRiyaz. Go on, treat yourself to a peek at some of his awesome collabs. You never know — you could be featured in his next one!

LIP-SYNC LEGENDS

From heartbreaking ballads to slick rap solos, TikTok is packed with lip-sync legends performing along with their favorite tracks. Here are some lip-syncing tips for you to try at home.

TOP TRACKS

If you want your video to go viral, choose a popular song. It'll make it easier for people to find it. Try browsing the available songs on TikTok, and then use the scissor icon to select the part of the song that you want.

CHOOSE RIGHT

Choosing a track that you already know the words to will make it easier to nail the lip-sync. To begin with, try choosing simpler songs without any fast rapping or talking. As you hone your lip-sync skills, you can tackle trickier tracks.

LISTEN AND LISTEN AGAIN

Once you have chosen the clip you want to use, listen to the words over and over again. Try not to sing along just yet, since you want to hear what the words to the song really are rather than what you might have thought they were.

LOOK IT UP

Not sure you heard those lyrics right? No problem. Look up your fave song online and you should be able to find the official lyrics, where you can check the words.

A LITTLE UNDERSTANDING

Do you know what all the lyrics mean? Understanding the lyrics and the emotion behind them will not only help you remember the words, but could also give you some choreography inspiration.

SING, SING, SING

Sing along to the clip. You've probably done this before, but try it again now that you are 100% sure of the lyrics.

MAGIC MOVES

Along with lip-syncing, videos are always more interesting with a bit of movement. Think about the lyrics and see what movements relate to the words you're miming. You may find that takes a bit of practice to get used to performing moves while you're trying to hold your phone!

WRITE THEM DOWN

Still forgetting the words? Don't sweat it. Write them down. A great way to learn something by heart is to write it down over and over again.

SNIP IT

If you're not happy with a lip-sync video you've recorded, you can edit it. Just go to "preview" and find the musical note and scissors icon. Play around with this to make the movement of your lips match up to the music.

The editing process is easier if you are in tune with the song and its rhythm as you record. Did you know that you can even record video at different speeds? So, you can slow down a really speedy song and smash it!

MEET ✔

@HOLLYH

🔍 ♫

Hang out with Holly H! Dubbed TikTok's biggest British star, this collab queen has performed with superstar Selena Gomez. Wow!

TIKTOK ACCOUNT: @hollyh
NAME: Holly Jo Hubert
DATE OF BIRTH: October 17, 1996
NATIONALITY: British
STAR SIGN: Libra
TALENTS: comedy and lip-syncing

INDIVIDUAL

Some of the best TikTok stars are the ones who aren't afraid to be themselves. That is certainly the case for Holly H. She embraces her quirks, and it's one of the reasons her fans love her.

HILARIOUS H

It's a well-known fact that Holly loves to laugh, but one thing she loves even more than that is making other people laugh. Holly's hilarious videos helped her gain tons of followers on Vine before she made the amazing move to TikTok, where her popularity has continued to grow.

BRIGHT BRITS

In 2020, the BRIT Awards (popular music awards in the UK) celebrated its 40th year with some of the hottest names in music. And next to them on the red carpet? TikTok stars Holly H and Tessa Bear (@tessa.bear). Holly was part of the BRITs Insider team, sharing all the behind-the-scenes action on the big night.

DOUBLE TROUBLE

There are simply too many incredible double acts to choose from, but here are a few of the best TikTok duos that everyone needs in their lives.

Zoe LaVerne and Cody Orlove

TIKTOK ACCOUNTS:
@zoelaverne and @codyorlove
NATIONALITY: American

This adorable couple are two of TikTok's most successful creators, and together they're even better! They have a YouTube channel where they share pranks, challenges, and even their fake wedding video.

Twin Melody

TIKTOK ACCOUNT: @twinmelody
NATIONALITY: Spanish

It's double the fun with Spain's singer-songwriter duo Twin Melody. Identical twins Aitana and Paula are known for their covers of Adele and Ed Sheeran as well as their awesome memes. They are proud members of the Twinnerz community, and have earned over 12 million followers. Their "Juju on Dat Beat" dance video was viewed over 30 million times.

The Rybka Twins

TIKTOK ACCOUNT: @rybkatwinsofficial
NATIONALITY: Australian

Teagan and Sam are Australia's mind-boggling, contorting Rybka Twins — you should see how flexible these gals are! Besides social media, the sisters appeared on *Australia's Got Talent*, and they've even got their very own book, *Twinning It*.

Lucas and Marcus Dobre

TIKTOK ACCOUNT: @dobretwins
NATIONALITY: American

Lucas and Marcus Dobre are twins with a joint TikTok channel. The boys post fantastic videos, which are mostly comedy skits, pranks, gymnastics, and vlogs!

The CroesBros

TIKTOK ACCOUNT: @croesbros
NATIONALITY: Aruban

Check out Gil and Jay's TikTok account, CroesBros. If you're not familiar with their videos, expect laugh-out-loud choreography and top-notch lip-syncing.

The Lopez Brothers

TIKTOK ACCOUNTS:
@tonylopez and @ondreazlopez
NATIONALITY: American

Say hello to dancing brothers Tony and Ondreaz. Before TikTok, these guys were already an established dancing duo and well-known on the competition circuit! Check out their amazing lip-sync and dance videos on TikTok!

TRENDING TRACKS

You can probably blame TikTok for getting a song or two stuck in your head! Discover the top tracks trending on the app, which inspire amazing memes, legendary lip-syncing, and daring dance routines.

"OLD TOWN ROAD" – LIL NAS X

Lil Nas X first uploaded the tune to TikTok himself, sparking a meme in which creators switch into Western outfits in time for the song's drop. It has since become the background music for just about anything, from backflips to baking.

"WOAH" – KRYPTO9095 FT. D3MSTREET

While the Woah dance move move was around long before TikTok, KRYPTO9095's viral song on the app introduced it to new Gen Z creators.

"LOTTERY" – K CAMP

The Renegade challenge swept TikTok in January 2020. The dance, which has around 15 complex moves (starting with the woah), is set to a short section of K Camp's "Lottery," where the word "renegade" is repeated several times. The dance was created by 14-year-old Jalaiah Harmon (@jalaiahharmon) on Instagram back in September 2019 before it was picked up on TikTok. Jalaiah's routine went viral, but her name didn't go with it. Instead, big TikTok stars like Charli D'Amelio and Addison Rae were known for doing it. Jalaiah finally got the recognition she deserved, later performing at the NBA All-Star Game and on *The Ellen DeGeneres Show*.

"TOOSIE SLIDE" – DRAKE

In April 2020, Drake's single went to number one on the Billboard Hot 100 Chart, bringing him to a tie with Mariah Carey for the most number one Hot 100 debuts. The song's success was most likely helped by the fact that Drake dropped a dance challenge on TikTok, creating a viral sensation.

"OBSESSED"– MARIAH CAREY

Following a video of TikToker @reesehardy_ crying while dancing to Mariah Carey's 2009 song, the track and dance went viral with millions of users following Reese's routine in their own videos.

GET LYRICAL

Scribble down your favorite songs, singers, and lyrics to inspire you!

YOU SAID WHAT?

TikTok isn't all about performing songs or dynamic dances. Check out these tips for performing and recording funny sound clips, from picking a quote to maximizing the comedy!

Where Do You Start?

TikTok is all about community, and it's cool to learn from one another! Taking a look at what other comedy creators are making is always a good place to begin. It'll give you some inspiration and help you come up with your own ideas.

What's Trending?

Look at the trending hashtags on the Discover page and see if there are any popular audio clips. Performing these tried-and-tested clips is a surefire way of getting followers.

Pick a Quote

Stuck trying to pick a quote that will make your followers laugh? If something makes you laugh, there's a good chance it'll make some of your followers chuckle, too! Think about whether you'll be able to record it easily — if it's dialogue between more than one person, you'll either need some friends to film it with, or you'll need to brush up on your TikTok editing skills.

Want to Make It Funnier?

Make your clip more interesting by using props. Look around your room for objects you could use to take your comedy to the next level.

Got the Moves

Will your video get people LOLing if you bring in some actions? The more acting you can bring in, the funnier your video.

Timing

Comedy is all in the timing. Make sure your lips move in time with the clip and that you know the words!

Wig Out!

Playing with your appearance really ups the entertainment factor of your quotes, and wigs are a quick and easy way of doing this. Choose a wig that is very different from your natural hair. TikTok comedy star Lauren Godwin uses wigs all the time to quickly change from one character to another.

Face It!

Nailing your facial expressions is key. The influencers who exaggerate their facial expressions and other body language are undoubtedly some of the funniest. Try practicing on your phone camera or in a mirror first!

Express Yourself

Some of the most successful comedy videos are unique and unusual, so don't get caught up trying to do exactly what other creators are doing. Staying true to yourself will help you stand out!

MEET
@JAYDENCROES

"**MY FAVORITE THING TO DO IS TO PUT A SMILE ON PEOPLE'S FACES!**"

#CROESBROS

He's the king of comedy and one half of the famous CroesBros . . . it's your turn to hang out with Jay Croes.

TIKTOK ACCOUNT: @jaydencroes
NAME: Jayden Croes
DATE OF BIRTH: November 11, 1998
NATIONALITY: Aruban
STAR SIGN: Scorpio
TALENT: comedy

SPREAD THE JOY

Jay says that his goal in life is to make people smile. If his huge amount of followers is anything to go by, it seems as though he's doing a seriously good job of reaching that goal.

FUNNY GUY

Jay portrays lots of hilarious characters across his channels. He often dresses up, and sometimes wears wigs as well. Jay has a unique style of his own — his colorful and quirky hairstyles and cool caps make him stand out.

BEST BROS

Some of Jay's most popular posts are the videos where he collaborates with his brother, Gil. Check out Gil's TikTok @gilmhercroes! The brothers also share a YouTube channel: CroesBros.

SUPER CELEBS

Here is a selection of fabulous celebrities with TikTok accounts. How many of them do you follow already?

@lewiscapaldi (Lewis Capaldi)

The best thing about Lewis's account is that he doesn't take himself too seriously. He likes poking fun at himself and he is super down-to-earth!

@jonasbrothers (The Jonas Brothers)

Nick, Joe, and Kevin share an account on TikTok for all their fans to enjoy the silly fun and games they get up to together.

@itsjojosiwa (JoJo Siwa)

Time to hang out with the upbeat explosion of talent and fun, JoJo Siwa. This gal's dance moves are made for TikTok. Expect neon colors, high ponytails, and plenty of LOLs.

@mackenzieziegler (Mackenzie Ziegler)

For plenty of cute dance videos plus appearances from her cool sis, Maddie, follow Mackenzie!

@joe_sugg (Joe Sugg)

For YouTuber fans out there, this one is for you! Joe Sugg is all over TikTok, so you can expect synchronized dance routines and plenty of laughs!

@niasioux (Nia Sioux)

Who doesn't love Nia? As you'd expect, she totally nails the dance TikTok genre.

@edsheeran (Ed Sheeran)

This megastar started his very own challenge, #BeautifulPeople. He encouraged fans to share videos with the hashtag. Keep spreading the positivity, Ed!

@dualipaofficial (Dua Lipa)

Her first post was viewed millions of times and involves her dancing to her song "Physical."

MEET @SKYANDTAMI

* COUPLE GOALS! *

#TRUELOVE

Sky and Tami are so adorable, and one of the cutest couples on TikTok. It's challenges galore for this comedy duo!

TIKTOK ACCOUNT: @skyandtami
NAME: Sky Odin
DATE OF BIRTH: January 10, 1990
NATIONALITY: Spanish
STAR SIGN: Capricorn
TALENTS: ballet dancing, modeling, comedy, and lip-syncing

NAME: Tama Tomo
DATE OF BIRTH: May 24, 1994
NATIONALITY: Spanish
STAR SIGN: Gemini
TALENTS: ballet dancing, modeling, comedy, and lip-syncing

TOP TEAM

This cute couple is a dream team! You only have to watch a handful of Sky and Tami's feel-good videos to see how much fun they have creating content together. Their dance routines are always perfectly in sync, and their challenge videos prove how much they trust each other. So much love!

Want to know how these two cuties create their daring moves and playful pranks? Well, they regularly share behind-the-scenes views of how they make their more complex clips.

FLIPPIN' AMAZING

You're casually watching one of their videos, thinking you know what's coming next, when all of a sudden . . . they throw in some serious acrobatics! The pair seamlessly weaves in cartwheels and flips without even breaking a sweat. How do they make it look that easy?

49

TIME TO DANCE

Now it's your turn to plan your own TikTok dance routine! You can use words or drawings to map out your moves.

Check out the awesome dance challenges trending on TikTok — there's always new inspo to get you moving!

Think about whether you want your moves to have people laughing or gasping in amazement. Comedy dances are awesome to watch!

TikTok tip!
Keep the moves simple to help you get them just right.

MEET

@STOKESTWINS

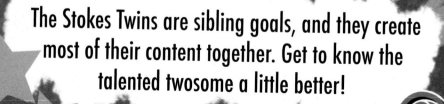

The Stokes Twins are sibling goals, and they create most of their content together. Get to know the talented twosome a little better!

TIKTOK ACCOUNT: @stokestwins
NAMES: Alex and Alan Stokes
DATE OF BIRTH: November 23, 1996
NATIONALITY: American
STAR SIGN: Sagittarius
TALENTS: acting, dancing, and comedy

FAMILY LIFE

These inseparable twins were born just two minutes apart (Alan is the oldest), and they're still super close! You can tell them apart by the small mole that Alex has on his face. They grew up in Hollywood, Florida. The boys love creating their videos together — it's what they do best!

SOCIAL SUCCESS

The Stokes Twins have built up a following on lots of social platforms. They have individual Instagram accounts, but they share TikTok. You can find their longer videos over on YouTube, where they are part of the YouTube group called Sunset Park.

SKATE BUDDIES

The twins are good friends with the skateboarder Ben Azelart, and the three of them have worked on several TikTok and YouTube videos together. Three is the magic number, and these boys love to create cool content!

TOTAL INSPO

Here are some thoughtful and inspirational TikTok stars who are putting their fame to good use by fighting for important causes.

Create for a Cause

TikTok's first ever collaborative charity program, #CreateForACause, took place in 2019. Creators came together to raise money for three charities:

- DoSomething
- Best Friends Animal Society
- Oceana

All users had to do was get creative using festive filters and post content using the hashtag. Easy! Over 1.4 million videos were created, and TikTok donated over $2 million to the chosen charities.

Anti-bullying

Jacob Sartorius has spoken out about how he has experienced bullying, and he wants to put a stop to it. He has told his young fans that they're not on their own.

"I know what it's like to be bullied . . . so, I just want to be one of the voices where people know that I went through that too . . . I was there."

Meet and greet

Charli D'Amelio has talked openly about the negativity that she has experienced since being in the spotlight. She didn't let it stop her from using TikTok, though, and she decided to spread some love instead. In 2019, Charli organized a meet and greet with her fans in her hometown dance studio to raise money for the Abilis Foundation, a charity that helps people with special needs and is very dear to Charli's heart.

Climate Change

TikTok has so many superstars who want to use their popularity for good, like Josh Richards! One of Josh's biggest passions is the environment. In January 2020, he spoke about climate change at the Consumer Electronics Show. He was part of a campaign that would award three fans $5,000, and all they had to do to enter was create a video about how they were helping to save the planet.

MEET
@BABYARIEL

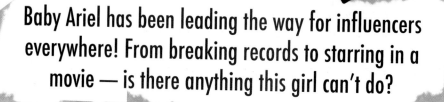

Baby Ariel has been leading the way for influencers everywhere! From breaking records to starring in a movie — is there anything this girl can't do?

TIKTOK ACCOUNT: @babyariel
NAME: Ariel Rebecca Martin
DATE OF BIRTH: November 22, 2000
NATIONALITY: American
STAR SIGN: Sagittarius
TALENTS: acting, singing

THE BIG TIME

If you want to find an influencer who's made history, Baby Ariel is your gal. She was the first Muser to reach over 20 million Musical.ly followers. Baby Ariel also has a successful career outside of TikTok. In 2020, she appeared in the Disney movie *Zombies 2*. If that wasn't enough, she starred in her own web miniseries called *Baby Doll Records* in 2018.

HARD TIMES

In 2015, Ariel's home flooded, and her family had to live out of suitcases at her grandparents' house. It was during that time that she downloaded the Musical.ly app. This difficult time for her family helped Ariel start a new career as a social media star.

ARIEL APPRECIATION

Ariel has created and shared a lot of great content, and she hopes to inspire her fans to get creative, too. But most important of all, Ariel uses her stardom to encourage others to be kind to each other on social media. You go, girl!

#HASHTAG TRENDING

There is a constant stream of new content being created every hour of every day! Here's our pick of the trends that went viral in the world of TikTok! Which ones do you LOVE the sound of?

1. HARIBO

The sweetest TikTok challenge! Back in 2019, David Kasprak posted a video set to Adele's "Someone Like You." In the clip, a gummy bear appears to be belting out the ballad, and when the video pans out, a whole chorus of gummy bears is seen to be singing along.

2. TRAVEL FROM HOME

In 2020, despite the global lockdowns, people were still able to travel . . . without leaving their living rooms. TikTok users came up with smart ways to take fake photos so that it appeared they were looking out of plane windows or were on a luxury vacation.

3. PEPPA PIG

When @beasinthetrap filmed himself eating a chocolate egg only to discover a Peppa Pig toy inside, Peppa became a TikTok sensation! TikTok users enjoyed the video so much that they started creating parodies of it!

4. SPOOKY DANCE

For this frightful challenge, TikTok users put on their finest skeleton costumes to perform dance routines to "Spooky Scary Skeletons" by Andrew Gold. It was a huge Halloween hit!

TikTok Tip!
It's fun to get your family and friends
involved with your TikTok challenges, too!

5. MAKE IT RAIN

Ever wished that you could
decide when it rains? TikTok
released a fun filter so that users
could do exactly that.

6. APRIL FOOL'S DAY

April 1 is the date in the calendar
that was legit made for TikTok
videos! Prepare to be amazed at
the level of creativity out there with
pranks and tricks galore.

7. TUMBLEWEED

This one is very easy but very
effective. Simply turn on some
beats and roll across the floor.
This challenge was started by talk
show host Jimmy Fallon.

8. NO HANDS

For this challenge, users need
both hands visible in the video,
so how do you hold up your
phone? Sounds tricky!

9. EAT ON THE BEAT

You can probably figure this one
out. It's eating food (any kind you
like) to the beat of a song.

10. AMERICAN IDOL

For this challenge, users
shared their amazing voice
with the world. The results
were astounding, with millions
of videos created and posted
online with the hashtag
#LikeAnAmericanIdol.

MEET ✓ @JACOBSARTORIUS

Singing, vlogging, and sharing his life on social media — welcome to the wonderful world of Jacob Sartorius!

Jacob has a cat named Prince. Cute!

TIKTOK ACCOUNT: @jacobsartorius
NAME: Rolf Jacob Sartorius
DATE OF BIRTH: October 2, 2002
NATIONALITY: American
STAR SIGN: Libra
TALENTS: lip-syncing, singing, and comedy

HOW IT ALL BEGAN .

Jacob started posting on Vine back in 2014. Superfans may remember that his first ever post there was an anti-bullying message! But it was his lip-sync videos on Musical.ly that brought Jacob serious attention and began building his fanbase. He's continued to build on his social media success on TikTok!

SUPER SONGS

Jacob's first single was called "Sweatshirt," and it was released in 2016 when he was only 13 years old. How amazing is that?! Since then, Jacob has proven that he's so much more than a one-hit wonder, continuing to perform for his fans and focusing on creating new music.

STARS IN HIS EYES

Jacob used to date the star of *Stranger Things*, Millie Bobby Brown. He was also rumored to be dating fellow TikTok star Baby Ariel, but they're just BFFs!

HELPING HANDS

Hands up if you love TikTok! Do you want some tips for getting your hand gestures on point? Here's a quick guide to doing just that, plus some all-important inspo to get you started!

The secret to TikTok is at your fingertips!

These tricks and hints will help you dazzle your followers with your amazing moves.

1. Start out by keeping the movements simple. It's better to nail a simple move than not quite hit a trickier one.

2. Practice. If you want to up your game, don't expect the moves to go right the first time you hit "Record." A few fails (or ten!) is all part of the fun.

3. Once you've picked your hand motions, it's time to try them out while holding your phone.

4. Angles are important in making your moves pop. Play around with holding your phone in different places to see what works best.

5. Move to the beat. Try to move in time with the music or sound that you're recording to!

Why don't you give the emoji hand-gesture challenge a try?

To complete the challenge, you'll need to add a series of hand emojis to the top of your screen for you to perform. And, as if that's not tricky enough, you have to time the sequence with a fast-paced dance track.

Like any big social media challenge, a bunch of celebs have taken a crack at it, including the Jonas Brothers.

NEED SOME IDEAS? HERE ARE SOME OF TIKTOK'S TRENDING HAND GESTURES TO GET YOU STARTED . . .

PEACE
If you hear the word "peace" in any lyrics, give this classic peace sign a try.

HAPPY
Point to your smile or pretend to draw one onto your face with your finger.

LATE
Tap your wrist like you're checking your watch.

SAD
Use your index finger to trace a tear from the edge of your eye, and down your face.

SHY
Touch both your index fingers together and pull your cutest doe-eyed face.

ROCKER HANDS
If you want to mime that you're rocking out, this hand gesture does the trick!

MEET  @ADDISONRE

Addison Rae is inspiring a generation with her talent for making TikTok videos that everyone is obsessed with!

TIKTOK ACCOUNT: @addisonre
NAME: Addison Rae Easterling
DATE OF BIRTH: October 6, 2000
NATIONALITY: American
STAR SIGN: Libra
TALENTS: dancing, gymnastics, and modeling

TEAMING UP

When Addison isn't busy collaborating with other social media stars like beauty guru James Charles, she's getting her family involved. Yep, her dad, Monty, and mom, Sheri, appear in many of her posts. In fact, videos with her parents often get the most hearts on TikTok.

ATHLETIC ADDISON

Addison is an all-action gal. She loves playing sports such as softball and volleyball, and she's a gymnast to boot. But that's not all! Addison is also a trained dancer and cheerleader.

STAR TALENT

As well as sharing her own videos, Addison has created content with some of the best TikTok talent on the planet, from Charli D'Amelio to JoJo Siwa. Addison is also signed with a talent agency — it looks like there will be big things to come for this TikTok star!

MEET @JOSHRICHARDS

Say hello to TikTok's one and only Josh Richards, a founding member of the Sway House collective!

Josh's second TikTok account is @uhhhjosh.

TIKTOK ACCOUNT: @joshrichards
NAME: Josh Richards
DATE OF BIRTH: January 31, 2002
NATIONALITY: Canadian
STAR SIGN: Aquarius
TALENTS: acting, dancing, and lip-syncing

THE BIG SCREEN

As well as being a social media influencer, Josh is also an actor. He already has some movies under his belt with his work on *Brother's Keeper* and *Summertime Dropouts*. One of his life goals is to work with his hero, Will Smith.

NO SWAY!

Josh became a member of Sway House in 2019 and left on a hiatus in May 2020. Sway House is an all-male creator collective where individual TikTok stars can get together to make content and share ideas. Make sure you check out the amazing videos the guys create: @theswayla.

GOOD DEEDS

One of Josh's biggest passions is the environment and fighting climate change. It's always inspiring to see stars using their platform to do something worthwhile, and that's exactly what Josh does! In January 2020, he spoke about climate change at the Consumer Electronics Show. (You can discover more about his speech on page 55.)

MEET @ZACHKING

The creator who's been bamboozling us with magical Tik-Tok videos! It's time to get to know Zach a bit better . . .

Zach has published three books, *Zach King: My Magical Life*, *Zach King: The Magical Mix-Up*, and *Zach King: Mirror Magic*.

TIKTOK ACCOUNT: @zachking
NAME: Zach King
DATE OF BIRTH: February 4, 1990
NATIONALITY: American
STAR SIGN: Aquarius
TALENTS: film editing and magic tricks

EDITING WIZARDRY

If you haven't heard of Zach King, here's what you need to know about the master of illusions. His mind-blowing videos are skilfully edited to look as though actual magic is happening on your screen. He calls his videos "digital sleight of hand," and they include everything from turning everyday objects into food to hands reaching through phone screens!

MAKEUP MAGIC

In March 2020, Zach collaborated with Selena Gomez, and the result was magical. Check it out! For the trick, Zach made it seem like a fan transformed into Selena using makeup. Zach pretended to be a makeup artist and asked a volunteer what kind of look they wanted. The woman showed Zach a picture of Selena on the cover of a magazine, and voilà! Her dreams came true. Zach cleverly edited the video, swapping in the real Selena at the end.

TAKE FLIGHT

One of Zach's most popular videos involves him flying around on a broomstick, just like Harry Potter. Nobody could figure out how he appeared to be hovering above the ground without any visible strings. Check it out and see what YOU think!

MAKE YOUR DAY

Imagine if you could hang out with Lil Huddy or dance with Charli D'Amelio! Choose which TikTok star you would want to join you on each of the activities on this page, and write your answers below.

You can pick from these suggestions, or choose your own!

Charli and Dixie D'Amelio

Lil Huddy

Lauren Godwin

Holly H

Maverick Baker

Who would you take to the movies?

_____

Got a secret? Which TikTok star would you trust with it?

_____

Who would you want by your side at dance class?

_____

If you wanted to have a good laugh with a TikTok star, who would you pick?

_____

Who would be your perfect homework buddy?

_____

Who would you like to spend time chilling out with?

_____

Who would be the most likely to cheer you up if you were having a bad day?

_____

You're bored. Who do you call?

_____

Feeling shy? Which of your favorite TikTok stars would you want to introduce you to their friends?

_____

You've changed schools. Who would you like to make friends with on your first day?

_____

MEET ✓ @LAURENGODWIN

She's TikTok's master of comedy, pranks, and parodies!

#

TIKTOK ACCOUNT: @laurengodwin
NAME: Lauren Godwin
DATE OF BIRTH: February 21, 2000
NATIONALITY: American
STAR SIGN: Pisces
TALENTS: comedy, pranks,
and impersonations

LAUGH OUT LOUD . . .

There are lots of comedy TikTok creators out there, but Lauren is one of the best! Lauren has been making content on the app since it was Musical.ly. She creates new content daily and keeps her fans entertained with hilarious TikTok videos.

HAIR-RAISING STYLE

Lauren's colorful and bubbly personality is reflected in her standout style — her hair color seems to be constantly changing! This comedy queen's wacky wardrobe helps her play lots of different characters, and she likes dressing up in various costumes and wigs.

PLAYFUL PRANKS

You can't celebrate Lauren without mentioning her outrageous pranks. Who remembers the one where Lauren pretends to drop her phone into a pool? It was viewed millions of times!

GOOD VIBES ONLY

Seen something awesome on TikTok that you want to remember? Jot it down right here! It might be a happy hashtag or a wonderful, wacky video. Whatever it is, make some notes.

If you're looking for inspiration for your next video or just want to increase the positivity in your life, you can look at this page!

TIKTOK CHECKLIST

You're almost ready to go! Use this handy list for a final check that you have everything you need to get started.

 Do you have your phone? You aren't going to get far without it. Make sure it has enough power if you're filming your clips out and about.

 Do you love your song/quote/routine? Loving what you are performing will really come across in your videos. If you love it, so will the rest of the world!

 Do you know all the words to your song? Is your choreography as polished as it can be? Practice makes perfect!

Is your location just right? Hold up your camera and, instead of looking at yourself, focus on what you can see behind you.

 Are you having a good time? TikTok is all about fun! If you aren't enjoying it, put down your phone and find something else to do. You shouldn't feel any pressure to share a video.

 Are you 18 years old or over? If you are, go ahead and make your TikTok account. If you're not, ask your parents for permission or keep working on your lip-sync and dance skills and you will be more than ready when that big birthday comes.

IT'S YOUR TIME TO
SHINE!

#MY TIKTOK

It's time for some fill-in fun! Plan your future TikTok account or write about one you already have. Don't forget to fill in your top-five lists, too. Ready, set . . . scribble!

@

My TikTok account: @ _____

My collaborations: _____

Write about your favorite collaborations with your friends or family.

_____

_____

Check off the types of videos you will make or write down some of your own amazing ideas.

◯ Lip-sync ◯ Dance ◯ Collab ◯ Pranks

My ideas:

_____

_____

I will make my videos in these places:

◯ my bedroom ◯ the backyard

◯ a park ◯ the playground

My ideas:

_____

_____

My fave hashtags:

1. _____

2. _____

3. _____

4. _____

5. _____

My top songs:

1. _____

2. _____

3. _____

4. _____

5. _____

IMAGE CREDITS